WORLD WILDLIFE FUND

Animal

ISBN: 0-7683-2033-X

Published in 1998 by Cedco Publishing Company, 100 Pelican Way, San Rafael, CA 94901.
For a free catalog of our entire line of books, write us at the address above or visit our website:
http://www.cedco.com or e-mail us at: *sales@cedco.com*

The Panda Device and WWF are registered trademarks.
Printed in Hong Kong.

Some photographs have been digitally-manipulated to produce this educational book.
Photo credits are listed in alphabetical order on the page noted.

front cover photo: © R. Andrew Odum/Peter Arnold, Inc. *title page*: © Jean-Paul Ferrero/AUSCAPE *end papers*: © Art Wolfe *owl*: © Henry H. Holdsworth
snakes: © James Carmichael/Image Bank *lemurs*: © Art Wolfe *pelicans*: © Jean-Paul Ferrero/AUSCAPE *wart hogs*: © Robin Brandt
kangaroos: © Mitchell Funk/Image Bank *flamingoes*: © Wolfgang Kaehler *polar bears*: © Robert Franz/Ron Kimball Stock Agency, © Art Wolfe
ostriches: © David W. Hamilton/Image Bank *dolphins*: © Brandon D. Cole, © Doug Perrine/Innerspace Visions
elephants: © Guido Rossi/Image Bank, © Kevin Schafer, © Art Wolfe *bee-eaters*: © Art Wolfe *giraffes*: Art Wolfe *macaws*: Art Wolfe
tree frogs: © R. Andrew Odum/Peter Arnold, Inc. *penguins*: © Kim Heacox/Peter Arnold, Inc., © Wolfgang Kaehler
impalas: © Charles and Rita Summers/Ron Kimball Stock Agency, © Rita Summers/Ron Kimball Stock Agency *eagles*: © Art Wolfe
zebras: © Martin Withers/Dembinsky Photo Associates, © Gunter Ziesler/Peter Arnold, Inc. *lions*: © Don Getty, © Wolfgang Kaehler, © Ron Kimball
Triptych: Composite from previous pages. Additional images include: © Jean-Paul Ferrero/AUSCAPE (kangaroo),
© Ron Kimball (lion), and © Guido Rossi/Image Bank (baby elephant).

123's

One owl

Two snakes

Three lemurs

Four pelicans

Five wart hogs

Six kangaroos

Seven flamingoes

Eight polar bears

Nine ostriches

Ten dolphins

Eleven elephants

Twelve bee-eaters

Thirteen giraffes

Fourteen macaws

Fifteen tree frogs

Sixteen penguins

Seventeen impalas

Eighteen bald eagles

Nineteen zebras

Twenty lions

5

9 10

15

19 20

3

4

8

13

14

7

18